MW01170287

Bright Kids Core Concepts Practice Test

Book Cover by: Carol Hampshire
Written and published by: Bright Kids NYC

Bright Kids NYC Inc.
www.brightkidsnyc.com
info@brightkidsnyc.com
917-539-4575

Table of Contents

About Bright Kids NYC

Bright Kids NYC was founded in New York City to provide language arts and math enrichment for young children and to educate parents about standardized tests through workshops and consultations, as well as to prepare young children for such tests through assessments, tutoring and publications. Our philosophy is that regardless of age, test-taking is a skill than can be acquired and mastered through practice.

At Bright Kids NYC, we strive to provide the best learning materials. Our publications are truly unique. First, all of our books have been created by qualified psychologists, learning specialists and teachers. Second, our books have been tested by hundreds of children in our tutoring, practice. Since children can make associations that many adults cannot, testing of materials by children is critical to creating successful test preparation guides. Finally, our learning specialists, and teaching staff have provided practical strategies and tips so parents can best help their child prepare to compete successfully on standardized tests.

Feel free to contact us should you have any questions or concerns.

Bright Kids NYC Inc.

Phone: 917-539-4575

Email: info@brightkidsnyc.com

www.brightkidsnyc.com

Core Concepts Practice Test ®

Introduction

Bright Kids NYC created the Core Concepts Practice Test to ensure that children are familiar with all core concepts that are key to succeeding on all standardized tests.

The Bright Kids Core Concepts Practice Test is based on the Bracken® Basic Concept Scale: Receptive (BBCS:R). This is an expanded version of the Bracken® School Readiness Assessment (BSRA), which is administered in various school districts and early childhood programs across the country.

The Bright Kids Core Concepts Practice Test can be used as a diagnostic to assess your child's abilities. Our Core Concepts Practice Test is not designed to generate a score or a percentile rank as the test has not been standardized with the actual BBCS:R or BSRA norms and standards. The objective of the practice test is to identify your child's strengths and weaknesses and test-taking ability so that you can prepare your child adequately for the actual test. Our Core Concepts Practice Workbook can be utilized prior to taking this practice test or afterwards to work on areas where your child needs the most help. The Answer Key includes the question type so that you can easily identify what type of core concept questions your child is struggling with.

In New York City, the Bracken® School Readiness Assessment (BSRA) is administered in conjunction with the OLSAT® for entry into the District and Citywide Gifted and Talented Programs. The BSRA covers core concepts such as colors, letters, numbers/counting, sizes/comparisons and shapes. The first five sections of the Bright Kids Core Concepts Test cover all of the BSRA subtests.

In order to maximize the effectiveness of the Bright Kids Core Concepts Practice Test, it is important to first familiarize yourself with the test and its instructions. In addition, it is recommended that you designate a quiet place to work with your child, ideally in a neutral environment free of noise and clutter. Finally, provide a comfortable and proper seating arrangement to enable your child to focus and concentrate to the best of his or her ability.

Children will be taking many standardized tests throughout their school years. Our philosophy is that regardless of age, test-taking is a skill than can be acquired and mastered through practice.

Bright Kids Core Concepts Practice Test Overview

Our Core Concepts Practice Test is based on the Bracken® Basic Concept Scale: Receptive (BBCS:R), which has a total of ten subtests and 158 questions.

The first five sections of our Core Concepts Practice Test focus on all the skills tested on the Bracken® School Readiness Assessment (BSRA), which is essentially the School Readiness Assessment portion of the BBCS:R. The BSRA is designed to evaluate children's knowledge of 85 fundamental academic concepts in the categories of colors, letters, numbers/counting, sizes/comparisons, and, shapes. The BSRA is typically administered to children ages three years to six years and eleven months. Just like the BSRA, the first five subtests of our Core Concepts Practice Test consists of colors, letters, numbers/counting, sizes/comparisons, and shapes subtests. There are a total of 87 items in the first five subtests.

The second part of the Bright Kids Core Concepts Test includes additional categories that are not on the Bracken School Readiness Test but are on the BBCS:R. We have included these concepts because the additional concepts that are on the BBCS:R are rigorously tested in many other aptitude tests like the Stanford-Binet® (direction/position, quantity, time/sequence) and the OLSAT (position/direction, and self/social awareness). In addition, these concepts are critical to success in any early childhood development program and need to be mastered by children entering kindergarten or early elementary grades.

While our Core Concept Workbook is based on the BBCS:R, we have improved it based on feedback from teachers, learning specialists and psychologists. We added new items that are not on the BBCS:R and utilized only items that are the most relevant for learning and for testing based on our extensive research. We renamed the position/direction, self/social awareness, quantity, and time/sequence sections as well as modified the content to make it more current and to better align it with the concepts that are utilized the most on all standardized tests.

Core concepts are an important part of language development for children and are deemed necessary to succeed in early formal education. The following core concepts are tested on our Core Concepts Test:

1. **Colors:** This subtest tests a child's knowledge of all primary and secondary colors.

2. **Letters:** This subtest includes both uppercase and lowercase letters.

3. **Numbers/Counting:** This subtest includes both single-digit and double-digit numbers. Children must be able to count items up to ten.

4. **Sizes/Comparisons:** This subtest includes one; two; and three-dimensional comparatives such as tall, short, and big or small. This measures a child's ability to match and compare objects based on their characteristics.

5. **Shapes:** This subtest includes one; two; and/or three-dimensional shapes as well as linear shapes, such as a curve.

6. **Direction/Position:** This subtest includes descriptions of the placement of an object relative to another such as below, above, inside, next to, over and under or placement of an object relative to itself, such as upside down or closed. It also includes the direction of the placement of an object such as left or right.

7. **Social Awareness (listed as Social/Self Awareness on BBCS:R):** This subtest includes emotional states such as happy, sad, angry, or mad.

8. **Texture/Material:** This subtest includes concepts such as wood, metal, rough, smooth, etc.

9. **Math Concepts (Listed as Quantity on the BBCS:R):** These concepts are critical to grasping fundamental math topics including descriptions of the degree to which objects exist and the space they occupy, such as double and full. This subtest also includes items that measure how children can manipulate quantity, e.g. less than and except.

10. **Time/Order (Listed as Time/Sequence on the BBCS:R):** This subtest includes concepts related to time and order such as fast, slow, third, and fourth.

In the Bright Kids Core Concepts Test, we cover all concepts on the BSRA in the first five subtests. However, on subtests six through ten, we are testing the most important concepts within each subtest that are common to all tests and those concepts children typically have the most difficulty with. Please note that the Bright Kids Core Concepts Workbook includes additional concepts and items within each subtest.

Bracken® Basic Concept Scale: Receptive (BBCS:R) Overview

The Bracken® Basic Concept Scale: Receptive (BBCS:R) consists of ten subtests that help evaluate a child's basic concept development, and the child's ability to express basic concepts that are core to learning. There are a total of 282 items on the BBCS:R:

1) Colors
2) Letters
3) Numbers/Counting
4) Sizes/Comparisons
5) Shapes
6) Direction/Position
7) Self/Social Awareness
8) Texture/Material
9) Quantity
10) Time and Sequence

The first five subtests makeup the School Readiness Composite, which measures educationally relevant concepts children need to master for formal early childhood education. These first five concepts are also tested on the Bracken® School Readiness Assessment (BSRA).

The BBCS:R is typically administered to children who are three years and zero months to six years and eleven months. The administration time is typically 30-40 minutes.

Table 1: Description of the BBCS:R

The items listed in bold are a part of the Bracken® School Readiness Assessment (BSRA).

Subtest	Description	Number of Items
Colors	Includes primary colors as well as secondary colors.	10
Letters	Includes uppercase and lowercase letters and sounds that correspond to letters.	15
Numbers/Counting	Contains single-digit and double-digit numbers (Numbers) and assigning a value to objects (Counting).	18
Sizes/Comparisons	Includes concepts that describe in one, two and three dimensions such as deep, short, long, big, and small. This subtest also tests a child's ability to match and compare objects based on common characteristics.	22
Shapes	Includes two-dimensional and three-dimensional shapes such as triangle and pyramid, as well as linear shapes such as a curve.	20
Direction/Position	Includes relational terms that describe spatial positioning of objects such as behind and in front of, or the positioning of an object relative to itself, like open, as well as a placement of an object such as right or middle.	62
Self/Social Awareness	Includes concepts referring to an emotional state of mind, such as happy and angry, as well as relative ages such as old and young.	33
Texture/Material	Includes concepts that describe salient characteristics of objects, such as hot and cold as well as the material composition of an object such as glass.	29
Quantity	Includes concepts that help identify quantity of objects such as more or less and space that objects occupy such as full or double.	43
Time/Sequence	Includes temporal items like night and day and sequential items such as first and third.	30

Core Concepts Practice Test ® Bright Kids NYC ©

Bracken® Basic Concept Scale: Receptive (BBCS:R) Administration

The BBCS:R starts with a few sample items to help familiarize the child with the structure of the test. The sample items can be prompted and explained as much as possible to ensure that the child has a good understanding of what is asked of him or her.

School Readiness Composite Score (SRC) Subtests 1-5

The subtests one through five on the BBCS:R create a School Readiness Composite Score (SRC). Correct answers are awarded one point and incorrect ones are given zero points. An individual subtest is discontinued if the child incorrectly answers three items in a row. The total score is the raw score for the SRC.

Subtests 6-10

Subtests six through ten have a different starting point for the subtests depending on the SRC score of the child. Then, all the subtests are administered until each subtest is complete or until the child obtains three consecutive zeros for each subtest.

For this section, a basal is also established. The basal is defined as the point in which a child answers three questions in a row correctly. If the child fails to answer three questions in a row correctly, the previous questions will be administered in reverse order until the child answers three consecutive questions correctly. Even if a basal is not established, all raw scores can still be converted into scaled scores. Scaled score is defined as the score that ranks a child relative to his or her peers based on norm-referenced age appropriate tables.

In order to scale a child's score relative to his or her peer group, the child's chronological age must be calculated by subtracting his or her birth date from the test date. When borrowing days from months, only 30 days is borrowed regardless of the length of the month. In addition, age is not rounded up or down to the nearest month. For example, if a child is tested on September 19th, 2010 and the child's birthday is September 20th, 2006, the child's chronological age is calculated to be 3 years, 11 months and 29 days.

The BBCS:R is normed in three-month age bands. This means that children born within the same three-month band will be compared to children only in that age band. For example, a child who is born January 4th, 2004 will be in the same group as a child born on March 15th, 2004, if they both take the test the same day, for example on January 5th, 2010. These children will both be normed with other children in the six years to six years and three months age band.

Composite Scores

There are two types of composite scores that can be obtained from the BBCS:R:

1) Receptive Total Composite (Receptive RTC)

   This is a measure of a child's use of all of the foundational concepts in all ten categories of the BBCS:R. Receptive Total Composite is calculated by adding the SRC scaled score (not the raw score) and the individual subtest scaled scores (6-10).

2) Receptive School Readiness Composite (Receptive SRC)

   The receptive SRC is an independent assessment of the child's school learning ability and is similar to the Bracken School Readiness Assessment (BSRA).

The composite scores can then be converted into percentile ranks. For example, if a child receives a 97% rank on the BBCS:R, this means that the child scored better than 97% of the children who took the test in his or her age band.

Bracken® School Readiness Assessment (BSRA) Overview

The Bracken® School Readiness Assessment (BSRA) is designed to evaluate children's knowledge of 85 fundamental academic concepts in the categories of colors, letters, numbers/counting, sizes/comparisons, and shapes. The BSRA is administered to children ages three years to six years and eleven months.

Table 2: Description of the BSRA

Subtest	Description	Number of Items
Colors	Includes primary colors as well as secondary colors.	10
Letters	Includes uppercase and lowercase letters.	15
Numbers/Counting	Contains single and double digit numbers (Numbers) and assigning a value to objects (Counting).	18
Sizes/Comparisons	Includes concepts that describe items in one, two, and three dimensions such as deep, short, long, big, and small. This subtest also tests a child's ability to match and compare objects based on common characteristics.	22
Shapes	Includes two-dimensional and three-dimensional shapes such as triangle and pyramid as well as linear shapes such as a curve.	20

BSRA General Administration Guidelines

The Bracken® School Readiness Assessment (BSRA) is typically administered in one sitting and takes about 15-20 minutes to administer and only includes the first five sections of our Core Concept Test:

- Colors
- Letters
- Numbers/Counting
- Sizes/Comparisons
- Shapes

There are four sample items. Three of the sample items include pantomime-like directions where the child practices pointing and showing items the examiner asks for. The last trial is from the Stimulus Book, where the tester asks the child to identify an item among four pictures. The children can ask to repeat an item and testers can repeat an item after 10 seconds if the child does not respond. Self-correction is allowed as long as it happens prior to administration of the next item. The child must only select one answer; if the child points to multiple items, the score will be counted as a zero.

All 85 items on the Bracken® School Readiness Assessment (BSRA) are scored one point for correct answers and zero points for wrong answers. If a child answers three questions in a row in a given subtest incorrectly, that subtest is immediately discontinued.

BSRA is also normed within three-month intervals. This means that children born within the same three-month band will be compared to children only in that age band. For example, a child who is born January 4th, 2004 will be in the same group as a child born on March 15th, 2004 if they both take the test on the same day, for example on January 5th, 2010. These children will both be normed with other children in the six years to six years and three months age band.

Just like in the BBCS:R, the raw scores are converted to scaled scores, which can then be converted to percentile ranks.

Core Concepts Practice Test ®

Bright Kids Core Concepts Practice Test Scoring Guidelines

The Bright Kids Core Concepts Practice Test can be scored only based on the total number of correct answers, or the overall raw score. Because this practice test has not been standardized with the BBCS:R or the BSRA, scaled scores or percentile ranks cannot be obtained from the raw score. Thus, it is important that this practice test is utilized as a learning tool to help evaluate a child's strengths and weaknesses rather than to estimate a scaled score or a percentile rank.

Core Concepts Practice Test ®

Getting Ready

Materials

1. The "Questions and Answers" section that is removed from this book.

2. Ideally, a "Do Not Disturb" sign for the room where you will be administering the test.

Prior to Testing

1. Familiarize yourself with the test and the instructions. Take the actual test to make sure that you can later explain to the child why certain answers are correct or incorrect.

2. Provide satisfactory physical conditions in the room where the child will be taking the test. Make sure that there is ample lighting and ventilation. Make sure that the table is clutter free and that the child and you can both sit comfortably at the table together.

3. To prevent interruptions, give the child the test when there are no other distractions in the house. If the house is not suitable, try to find a local library or a school.

During Testing

1. Make sure that the child is comfortable with pointing to only one answer. Use pantomime directions such as, "Point to the nose" or "ears" or "the book" to make sure the child understands what pointing means.

2. Ask all questions exactly as it is written; do not paraphrase or change the questions.

3. Do not give the child any feedback during testing. Discuss the answers only after testing is complete.

4. Always provide positive reinforcements to ensure that the child completes the task. If he or she slows down or wants to give up, provide encouragement and support.

5. Administer breaks at the end of each section as needed. The test can even be completed in two sittings. The first five sections, which constitute the BSRA, can be administered in one sitting and the rest can be administered at another time or on another day.

Core Concepts Practice Test ®

Instructions

Please remember to detach the "Questions and Answers" pages. Put the book in front of the child and instruct him or her to keep the book closed until you are both ready to start. Then, turn to the first question of the test that has the clown holding balloons and begin administration. Write "1" for each correct answer and "0" for each incorrect answer on the "Questions and Answers" pages.

Questions and Answers

Core Concepts Practice Test ®

Section 1: Colors

SAY: Look at the picture with the clown. Point to the color that is…

ITEM	QUESTION	CHILD'S ANSWER	SCORE (1 or 0)
Items 1-10			
1.	blue		
2.	orange		
3.	purple		
4.	red		
5.	yellow		
6.	white		
7.	black		
8.	brown		
9.	pink		
10.	green		

Section 2: Letters

SAY: Look at the letters. Point to the…

ITEM	QUESTION	CHILD'S ANSWER	SCORE (1 or 0)
Items 1-2			
1.	C		
2.	K		
Items 3-4			
3.	P		
4	Z		
Items 5-6			
5.	M		
6.	W		
Items 7-8			
7.	J		
8.	B		
9.	g		
10.	n		
Items 11-13			
11.	s		
12.	f		
13.	t		
Items 14-17			
14.	x		
15.	q		
16.	l		
17.	d		

Section 3: Numbers/Counting

SAY: Look at all the pictures. Point to the…

ITEM	QUESTION	CHILD'S ANSWER	CORRECT ANSWER	SCORE (1 or 0)
Items 1-5				
1.	zero		-	
2.	nine		-	
3.	eight		-	
4.	five		-	
5.	three		-	
Items 6-10				
6.	one		-	
7.	two		-	
8.	five		-	
9.	four		-	
10.	six		-	
Items 11-13				
11.	85		-	
12.	33		-	
13.	91		-	
Items 14-16				
14.	49		-	
15.	17		-	
16.	51		-	
17.	three cats		1	
18.	six frogs		1	
19.	seven fish		2	
20.	five ladybugs		2	

Section 4: Sizes/Comparisons

SAY: Look at the pictures and answer the questions.

ITEM	QUESTION	CHILD'S ANSWER	CORRECT ANSWER	SCORE (1 or 0)
1.	Which house is small?		2	
2.	Which fish is large?		2	
3.	Which insects are different?		1	
4.	Which gloves match?		4	
5.	Which animal has a short tail?		2	
6.	Which socks are the same?		3	
7.	Which tree is tall?		1	
8.	Which pool is deep?		2	
9.	Which vegetables do not match?		3	
10.	Which box is large?		3	
11.	Which road is narrow?		4	
12.	Which vases are unequal?		3	
13.	Which water is shallow?		1	
14.	Which glasses are of equal size?		3	
15.	Which person is thin?		3	
16.	Which bridge is wide?		2	
17.	Which hat fits exactly?		3	
18.	Which person is doing something other than playing an instrument?		3	
19.	Which dog has long hair?		2	
20.	Which doll is little?		2	
21.	Which cars are alike?		1	
22.	Which balls are exactly the same?		2	
23.	Which fish are similar?		1	

Core Concepts Practice Test ® Bright Kids NYC ©

Section 5: Shapes

SAY: Look at all the pictures. Point to the…

ITEM	QUESTION	CHILD'S ANSWER	CORRECT ANSWER	SCORE (1 or 0)
Items 1-7				
1.	heart		3	
2.	circle		8	
3.	rectangle		4	
4.	diamond		5	
5.	square		7	
6.	oval		6	
7.	triangle		1	
8.	soccer players in a line		1	
9.	star		3	
Items 10-12				
10.	cylinder		3	
11.	pyramid		1	
12.	cube		4	
13.	turtles in a row		1	
14.	curve		3	
15.	arch		1	
16.	two diagonal lines		4	
17.	angle		1	

Section 6: Direction/Position

SAY: Look at all the pictures. Point to the…

ITEM	QUESTION	CHILD'S ANSWER	CORRECT ANSWER	SCORE (1 or 0)
1	bird on top of the cage		1	
2.	car next to the motorcycle		3	
3.	flowers inside the vase		1	
4.	stars above the moon		4	
5.	dog in between the two trees		1	
6.	cat under the chair		2	
7.	child beside the house		1	
8.	person high on the ladder		1	
9.	child that is upside down		3	
10.	sun below the clouds		3	
11.	cat furthest away from the tree		4	
12.	child sitting across from the adult		3	
13.	children walking towards each other		1	
14.	flowers that are together		3	
15.	low flying kite		1	
16.	child turning left		1	
17.	ball in the middle of the table		1	

Core Concepts Practice Test ®   Bright Kids NYC ©

Section 7: Social Awareness

SAY: Look at all the pictures. Point to the…

ITEM	QUESTION	CHILD'S ANSWER	CORRECT ANSWER	SCORE (1 or 0)
Items 1-2				
1.	laughing child		2	
2.	crying child		1	
Items 3-4				
3.	sad child		2	
4.	happy child		1	
Items 5-6				
5.	child that is afraid		1	
6.	child that is excited		3	
7.	person who is frowning		4	
8.	child who is relaxing		3	
9.	sleepy cat		1	
10.	worried mother		1	

Section 8: Texture/Material

SAY: Look at all the pictures. Point to the…

ITEM	QUESTION	CHILD'S ANSWER	CORRECT ANSWER	SCORE (1 or 0)
Items 1-2				
1.	one that is hot		3	
2.	one that is cold		1	
Items 3-4				
3.	one made of metal		2	
4.	one made of glass		1	
5.	one that is sharp		1	
6.	one made of wood		1	
7.	rough water		1	
8.	one that is smooth		1	
9.	one that is dull		1	
10.	tight rope		1	

Section 9: Math Concepts

SAY: Look at all the pictures. Point to the…

ITEM	QUESTION	CHILD'S ANSWER	CORRECT ANSWER	SCORE (1 or 0)
1.	cats that are both asleep		1	
Items 2-3				
2.	half cookie		2	
3.	quarter cookie		4	
Items 4-5				
4.	squirrel with the most nuts		3	
5.	squirrel with the least nuts		1	
Items 6-7				
6.	empty bowl		2	
7.	bowl with some cereal		1	
8.	vase with the fewest flowers		1	
9.	branch with a single bird		3	
Items 10-11				
10.	monkey with the greatest number of bananas		1	
11.	monkey with the least number of bananas		2	
12.	bowl with a few fish		3	
Items 13-14				
13.	double scoop of ice cream		1	
14.	triple scoop of ice cream		3	
15.	pair of gloves		1	
16.	whole pizza		3	
17.	child who has more lollypops than the others		1	
18.	cup that has no juice left		4	
19.	couple of goldfish		2	
Items 20-21				
20.	plus sign		1	
21.	minus sign		4	
22.	child taking another cookie		2	
23.	dozen crayons		1	
24.	child who has as many balloons as the other		3	
25.	part of the banana		3	
26.	kid who neither has a train nor a ball		4	

Section 10: Time/Order

SAY: Look at all the pictures. Point to the…

ITEM	QUESTION	CHILD'S ANSWER	CORRECT ANSWER	SCORE (1 or 0)
Items 1-2				
1.	child sitting in the third row		3	
2.	child sitting in the first row		1	
Items 3-4				
3.	dog that is eating second in line		4	
4.	dog that eating fourth in line		2	
Items 5-6				
5.	rightmost bird that is about to fly		1	
6.	leftmost bird that is about to fly		4	
Items 7-8				
7.	one that shows spring		4	
8.	one that shows winter		2	

Bright Kids
Core Concepts Practice Test

Core Concepts Practice Test ®

Section 1: Colors

Core Concepts Practice Test ®

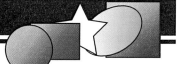

Items 1 - 10

Core Concepts Practice Test ®

Section 2: Letters

Items 1 and 2

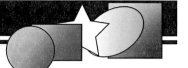

Items 3 and 4

Items 5 and 6

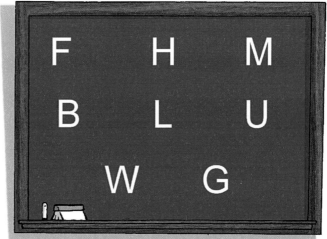

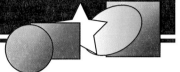

Items 7 and 8

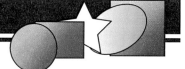

Item 9

j   g   l   o

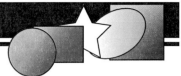

Item 10

m   p   b   n

Core Concepts Practice Test ®   Bright Kids NYC ©

Core Concepts Practice Test ® Bright Kids NYC ©

Section 3: Numbers/Counting

Core Concepts Practice Test ®

Items 6 - 10

Core Concepts Practice Test ®

Bright Kids NYC ©

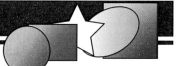

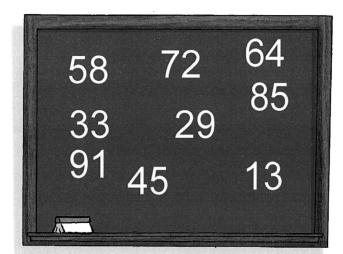

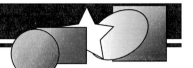

Items 14 - 16

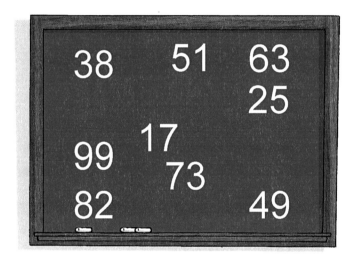

Core Concepts Practice Test ®

Bright Kids NYC ©

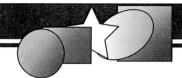

Item 17

1

2

3

4

Item 18

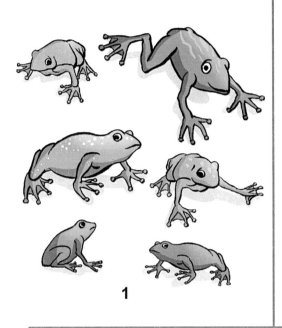

1

2

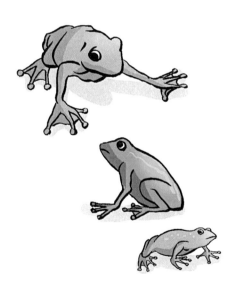

3

4

Core Concepts Practice Test ®

Item 19

1

2

3

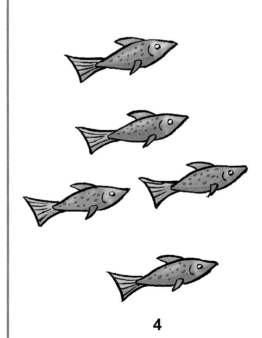

4

Item 20

1

2

3

4

Section 4: Sizes/Comparisons

Core Concepts Practice Test ®

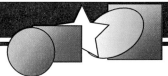

Item 1

1

2

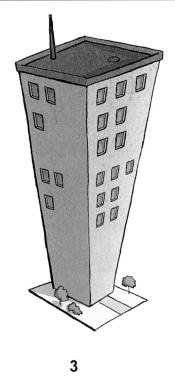

3

4

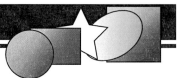

Item 2

1

2

3

4

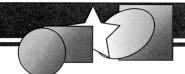

Item 3

1

2

3

4

Core Concepts Practice Test ®

Item 4

1

2

3

4

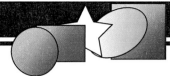

Item 5

1

2

3

4

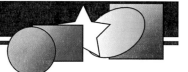

Item 6

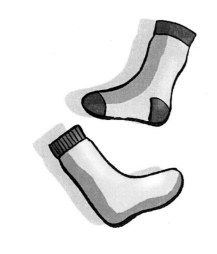

1

2

3

4

Core Concepts Practice Test ®

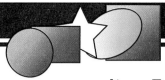

Item 7

1

2

3

4

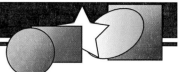

Item 8

1

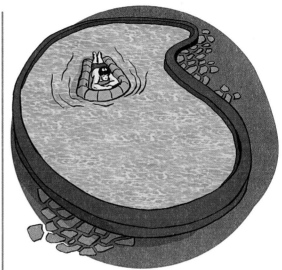

2

3

4

Core Concepts Practice Test ®

Item 9

1

2

3

4

Item 10

1

2

3

4

Core Concepts Practice Test ®

Bright Kids NYC ©

Item 11

1

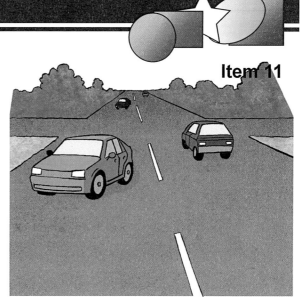

2

3

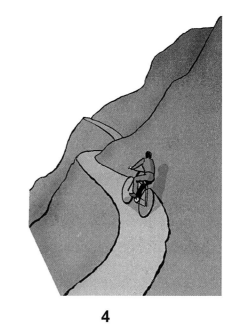

4

Core Concepts Practice Test ®

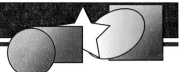

Item 12

1

2

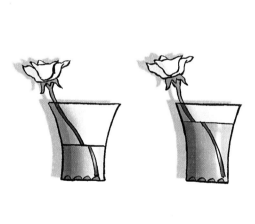

3

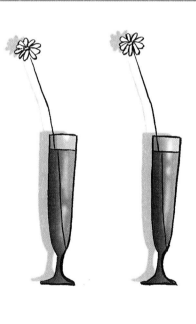

4

Core Concepts Practice Test ®

Bright Kids NYC ©

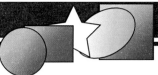

Item 13

1

2

3

4

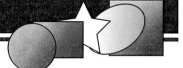

Item 14

1

2

3

4

Core Concepts Practice Test ® Bright Kids NYC ©

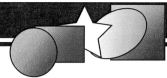

Item 15

1

2

3

4

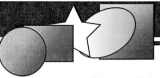

Item 16

1

2

3

4

Core Concepts Practice Test ®

Bright Kids NYC ©

Item 17

1

2

3

4

Item 18

1

2

3

4

Core Concepts Practice Test ®

Item 19

1

2

3

4

Item 20

1

2

3

4

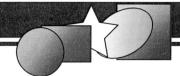

Item 21

1

2

3

4

Item 22

1

2

3

4

Core Concepts Practice Test ®

Bright Kids NYC ©

Item 23

1

2

3

4

Section 5: Shapes

Items 1 - 7

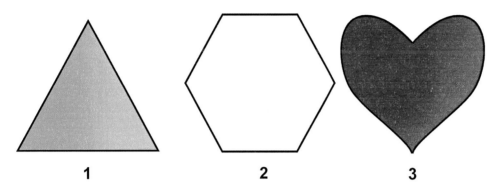

1   2   3

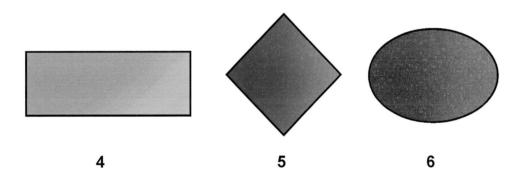

4   5   6

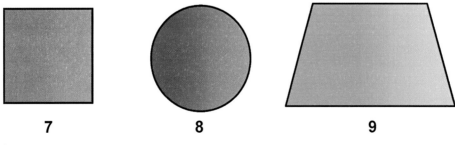

7   8   9

Item 8

1

2

3

4

Core Concepts Practice Test ® Bright Kids NYC ©

Item 9

1

2

3

4

Items 10 - 12

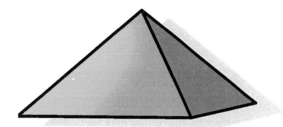

1

2

3

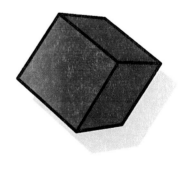

4

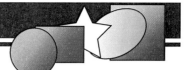

Item 13

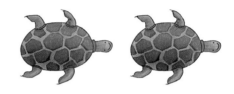

1

2

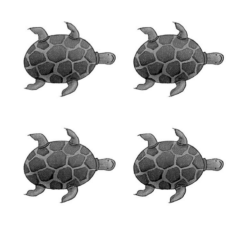

3

4

Item 14

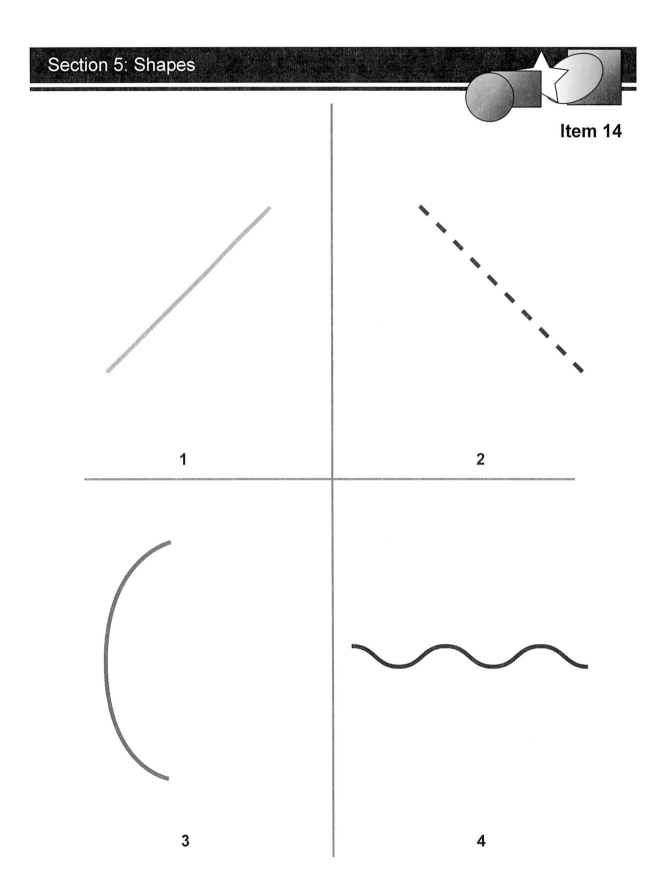

1

2

3

4

Core Concepts Practice Test ®

Bright Kids NYC ©

Item 15

1

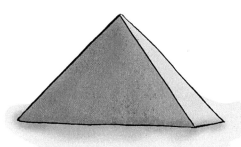

2

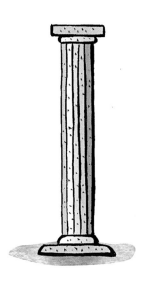

3

4

Item 16

1

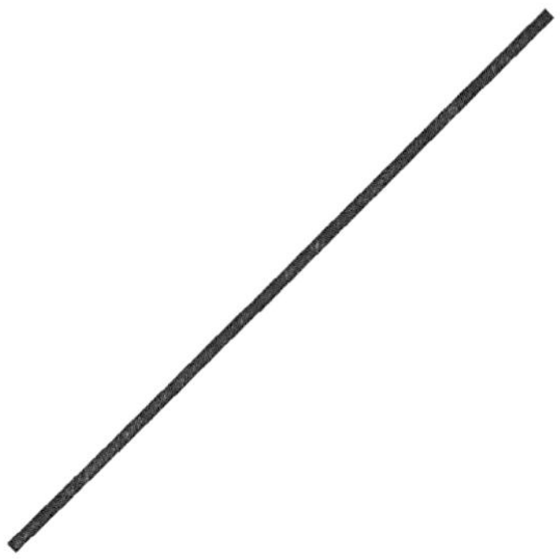

2

3

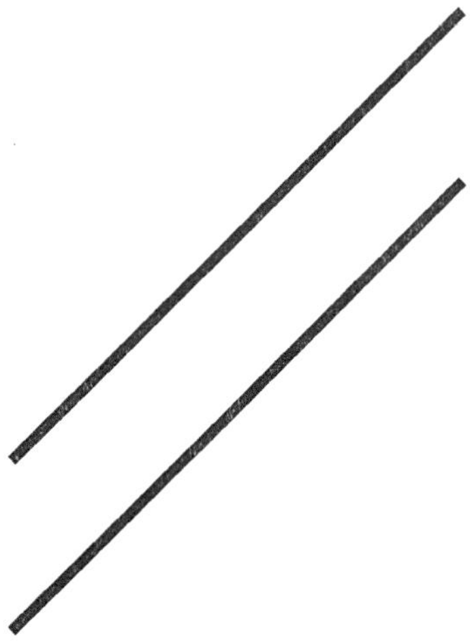

4

Core Concepts Practice Test ®

Bright Kids NYC ©

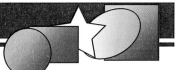

Item 17

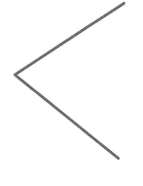

1

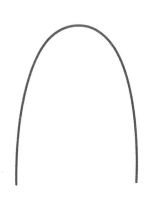

2

3

4

Section 6: Direction/Position

Item 1

1

2

3

4

Item 2

Item 3

1

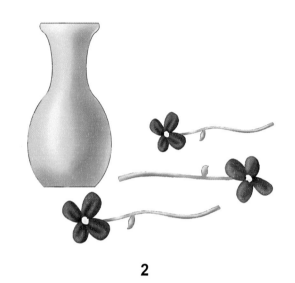

2

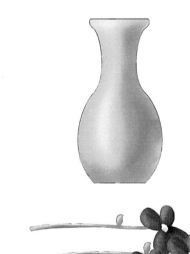

3

4

Core Concepts Practice Test ®

Item 4

1

2

3

4

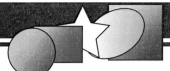

Item 5

1

2

3

4

Item 6

1

2

3

4

Core Concepts Practice Test ®

Bright Kids NYC ©

Item 7

1

2

3

4

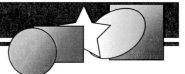

Item 8

1

2

3

4

Core Concepts Practice Test ® Bright Kids NYC ©

Item 9

1

2

3

4

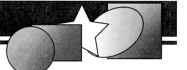

Item 10

1

2

3

4

Item 11

1

2

3

4

Core Concepts Practice Test ®

Item 12

1

2

3

4

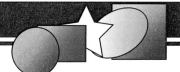

Item 13

1

2

3

4

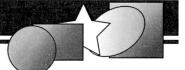

Item 14

1

2

3

4

Core Concepts Practice Test ®

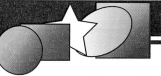

Item 15

1

2

3

4

Core Concepts Practice Test ®

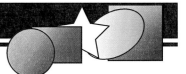

Item 16

Core Concepts Practice Test ®

Item 17

1

2

3

4

Core Concepts Practice Test ®

Section 7: Social Awareness

Core Concepts Practice Test ®

Items 1 and 2

1

2

3

4

Items 3 and 4

1

2

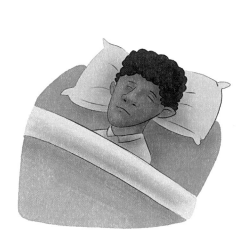

3

4

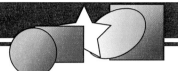

Items 5 and 6

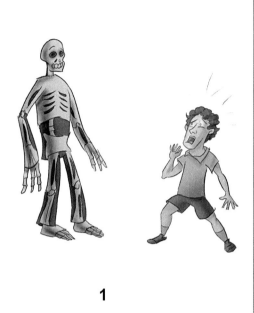

1

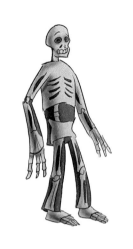

2

3

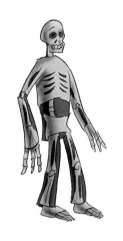

4

Item 7

1

2

3

4

Core Concepts Practice Test ®

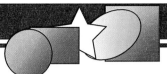

Item 8

1

2

3

4

Item 9

1

2

3

4

Core Concepts Practice Test ®

Bright Kids NYC ©

Item 10

1

2

3

4

Section 8: Texture/Material

Core Concepts Practice Test ®

Items 1 and 2

1

2

3

4

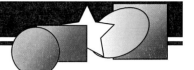

Items 3 and 4

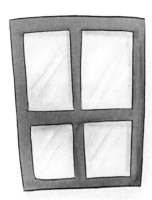

1

2

3

4

Item 5

1

2

3

4

Item 6

1

2

3

4

Core Concepts Practice Test ®

Bright Kids NYC ©

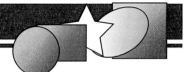

Item 7

1

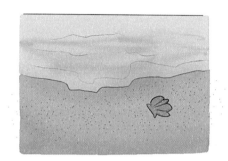

2

3

4

Core Concepts Practice Test ®

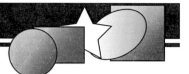

Item 8

1

2

3

4

Core Concepts Practice Test ® Bright Kids NYC ©

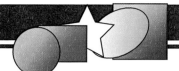

Item 9

1

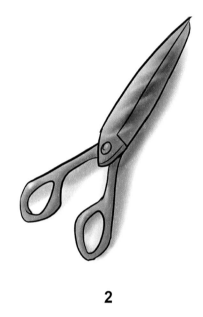

2

3

4

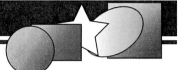

Item 10

1

2

3

4

Section 9: Math Concepts

Item 1

1

2

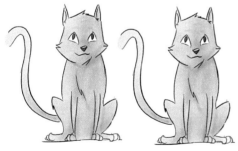

3

4

Items 2 and 3

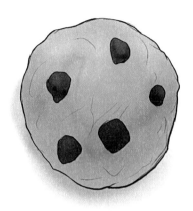

1

2

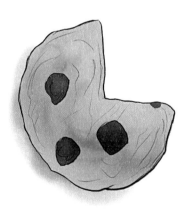

3

4

Core Concepts Practice Test ®

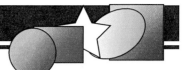

Items 4 and 5

1

2

3

4

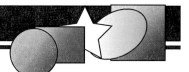

Items 6 and 7

1

2

3

4

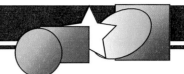

Item 8

1

2

3

4

Item 9

1

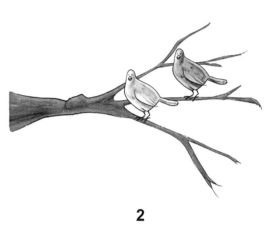

2

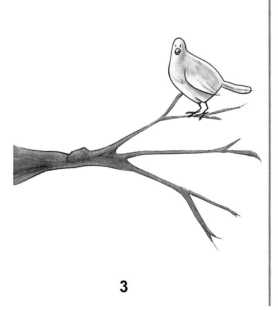

3

4

Items 10 and 11

1

2

3

4

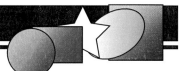

Item 12

1

2

3

4

Core Concepts Practice Test ®

Bright Kids NYC ©

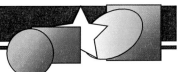

Items 13 and 14

1

2

3

4

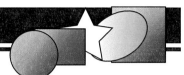

Item 15

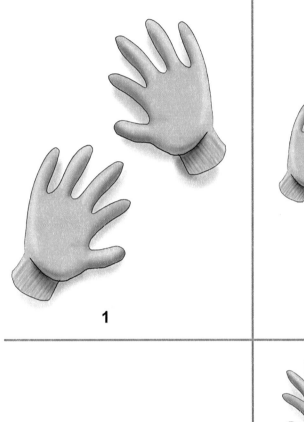

1

2

3

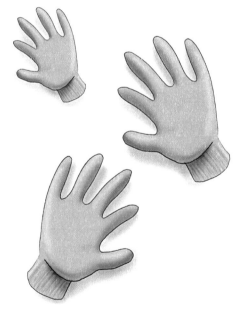

4

Core Concepts Practice Test ®

Bright Kids NYC ©

Item 16

1

2

3

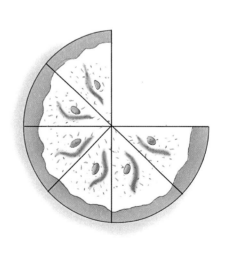

4

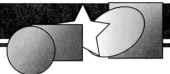

Item 17

1

2

3

4

Core Concepts Practice Test ®

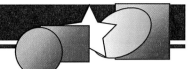

Item 18

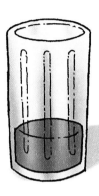

1

2

3

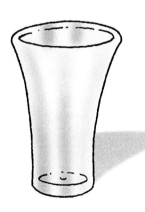

4

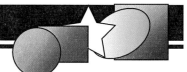

Item 19

1

2

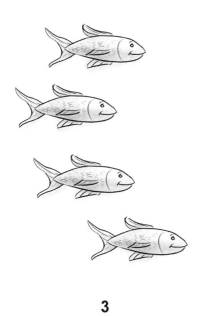

3

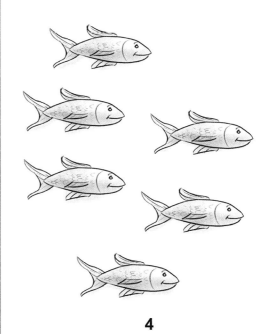

4

Core Concepts Practice Test ®

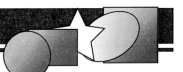

Items 20 and 21

1

2

3

4

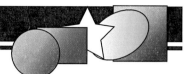

Item 22

1

2

3

4

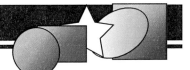

Item 23

1

2

3

4

Item 24

1

2

3

4

Core Concepts Practice Test ®

Bright Kids NYC ©

Item 25

1

2

3

4

Item 26

1

2

3

4

Core Concepts Practice Test ®

Section 10: Time/Order

Core Concepts Practice Test ®

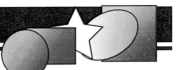

Items 1 and 2

1   2

3   4

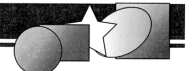

Items 3 and 4

1

3

2

4

Core Concepts Practice Test ®

Bright Kids NYC ©

Items 5 and 6

1

2

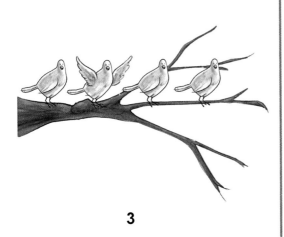

3

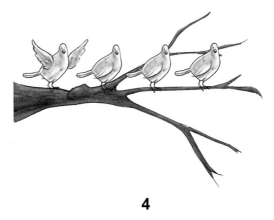

4

Items 7 and 8

1

2

3

4

Core Concepts Practice Test ®

Bright Kids NYC ©